The Chunnel

THE BUILDING OF A 200-YEAR-OLD DREAM

Jil Fine

HIGH
interest
books

Children's Press®
A Division of Scholastic Inc.
New York / Toronto / London / Auckland / Sydney
Mexico City / New Delhi / Hong Kong
Danbury, Connecticut

Book Design: Michelle Innes and Erica Clendening
Contributing Editor: Matt Pitt
Photo Credits: Cover, title page, p. 3 © Philippe Caron/Corbis Sygma;
p. 4 © MAPS.com/Corbis; p. 6 © AP/Wide World Photos; pp. 8–9
Thomee de Gamond/NATIONAL ARCHIVES OF CANADA/C-062728;
pp. 11, 18–19 akg-images; p. 12 © Hulton-Deutsch Collection/Corbis;
pp. 14–15 © Polak Matthew/Corbis Sygma; p. 16 © Joe McDonald/Corbis;
pp. 21, 27, 29, 30, 31-32, 34 Jim Byrne QAPHOTOS; p. 24 © Jacques
Langevin/Corbis Symga; p. 37 © Tim Graham/Corbis; p. 39 © Reuters
NewMedia Inc./Corbis; p. 40–41 © Colin Garratt; Milepost 92 ½/Corbis

Library of Congress Cataloging-in-Publication Data

Fine, Jil.
  The Chunnel : the building of a 200-year-old dream / by Jil Fine.
  p. cm.—(Architectural wonders)
  Summary: Discusses the history, purpose, and construction of the
  Chunnel, a railroad tunnel that crosses the English Channel, uniting
  England and France.
  ISBN 0-516-24077-3 (lib. bdg.)—ISBN 0-516-25906-7 (pbk.)
  1. Channel Tunnel (England and France)—Juvenile literature. [1.
  Channel Tunnel (England and France) 2. Railroad tunnels—English
  Channel. 3. Tunnels—Design and construction.] I. Title. II. Series.

TF238.C4F56 2003
624.1'94'0916336—dc22
                                    2003012312

  2 3 4 5 6 7 8 9 10 R 13 12 11 10 09 08 07 06

Contents

Introduction

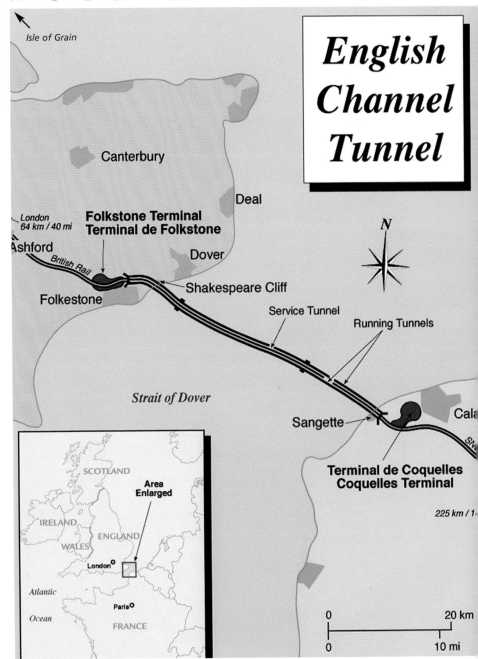

Isle of Grain

Canterbury

Deal

London
64 km / 40 mi

Folkstone Terminal
Terminal de Folkstone

Ashford

British Rail

Dover

Folkestone

Shakespeare Cliff

Service Tunnel

Running Tunnels

Strait of Dover

Sangette

Cala

Terminal de Coquelles
Coquelles Terminal

225 km / 1

N

English Channel Tunnel

SCOTLAND

Area Enlarged

IRELAND

ENGLAND

WALES

London○

Atlantic

Ocean

Paris○

FRANCE

0   20 km

0   10 mi

One hundred and fifty feet (45.7 meters) below the bottom of the English Channel, the noise is unbearably loud. A massive tunnel-boring machine (TBM) has been working nonstop for days. It is ripping up clay that has been here for thousands of years. Nearby, five miners are using jackhammers to dig into the clay. The miners haven't seen light for six hours. These workers have been digging under the English Channel for the past two years. One worker pauses for just a moment. Sweat is dripping down his face and neck. He takes a long drink of water and goes back to work.

People had been dreaming of building a tunnel under the English Channel for two hundred years. The Chunnel is the result of their dreams. This tunnel allows people to cross the choppy waters of the English Channel in less than thirty minutes. It also unites two nations—England and France.

Why were thousands of people devoted to this project? Why would they work so hard and risk so many personal dangers to complete it? Why were two hundred banks willing to give money to build the Chunnel? This project was a wonder of engineering, patience, and willpower. This is the story of how it became a reality.

This map shows where the Channel Tunnel connects, and what it looks like. As the inset map shows, the Chunnel was built at the narrowest point of separation between England and France.

chapter one

A Rough Start

In 1971, dense fog led to an explosion between this fuel tanker and a cargo ship from Peru. The explosion sent crew members flying.

For hundreds of years, the English Channel has served as an important link between England and the rest of Europe. Countless ships traveled back and forth to trade goods. The armies of several European nations also crossed the channel to invade England.

The English Channel is not a very large body of water. It measures only 112 miles (180 kilometers) wide. However, its waters are very rough. High winds and strong tides make crossing the Channel very difficult. Fog is also very common on the Channel, making trips even riskier.

Sometimes ship crews learned of the Channel's dangers firsthand. On January 11, 1971, a tanker smashed into a freighter. Nine people died. The tragedy didn't end there. The next morning, a German ship struck the wreckage. It sank too, and seventeen more lives were lost.

Changing the Channel

Records show that ideas for building a tunnel beneath the Channel began around 1802. However, most of these early designs were not well planned.

Starting in 1834, Frenchman Aimé Thomé de Gamond began to take a serious interest in linking England to France. With each passing year, Thomé's

devotion to the project grew. He spent years of his life and nearly his entire fortune trying to develop an easier way to cross the Channel. He designed several plans. One of his dreams was to build an iron tunnel. Five other plans focused on building a bridge across the water. Thomé even had a plan to construct an artificial island. He hoped to place railways and shipping ports around the island, which would make traveling easier.

Although his early plans didn't work out, Thomé de Gamond's passion and ideas drove many men and women to dream about a tunnel beneath the English Channel.

In 1855, Thomé even risked death to make his dream come true. Thomé claimed that he swam to the bottom of the Channel. That's a dive of over 108 feet (33 m)! He said that he used bags of stones to help him sink. Once he reached the bottom, he collected samples of the sea floor. Then he inflated ten pig bladders to help lift him back to the surface. Whether Thomé's story was true or a tall tale, no one knows for sure.

In time, others grew excited by Thomé's plans. Even England's Queen Victoria approved of his work. In 1870, however, just as he thought his plans had enough support, the Franco-Prussian War began. France went to war with what is now part of Germany. The French put all their attention toward the war. Thomé died a few years later, in 1876.

The First Dig

In 1875, a great advance was made in tunnel digging. British Colonel Frederick E. Beaumont invented a tunnel-boring machine (TBM). Beaumont's invention had two arms in the front of it. These arms—which looked like an airplane's propeller—cut through earth as they spun. They could shred one inch (2.5 centimeters) of earth a minute. A system of buckets moved this earth to the back of the machine. The TBM ran on compressed air. This air would in turn provide fresh oxygen for tunnel workers.

Beaumont believed that his new machine would make an English Channel tunnel a reality. A British railroad owner named Sir Edward Watkin agreed. In 1881, Watkin started tunneling with his own TBM on Shakespeare Cliff, England. This cliff overlooks the Channel.

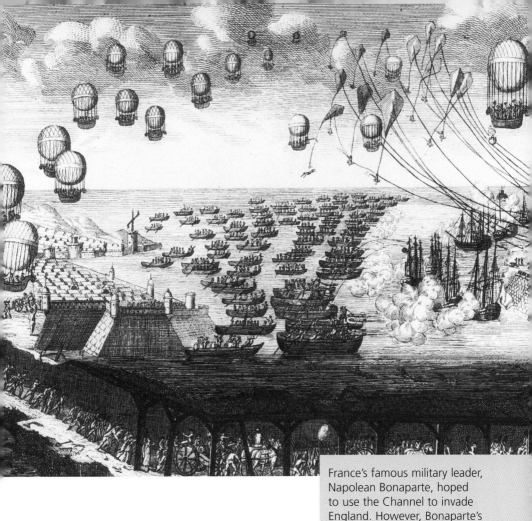

France's famous military leader, Napolean Bonaparte, hoped to use the Channel to invade England. However, Bonaparte's plan to carry his armies using balloons never happened.

Watkin's work won the support of both the French and British governments. The French also began to dig. Watkin had hopes of finishing a small tunnel within five years. However, many people in England wanted Watkin to stop his work. They were worried that nations such as Germany or France

Many generations of British men and women opposed the Chunnel out of worry that other nations would use it to invade England. In 1955, British defense minister Harold Macmillan declared that building a tunnel would not increase the risk of invasion.

might use the tunnel to invade England. Some people imagined that thousands of soldiers, dressed in ordinary clothes, might ride a train in the tunnel to enter the country. Once they reached England's shores, they would be able to launch an attack. Watkin tried to change the critics' minds, but could not. Watkin's TBM stopped digging on August 12, 1882. It had drilled 6,178 feet (1,883 m). The French continued digging for a few months more. Their TBM had made 5,476 feet (1,669 m) of progress.

Changing Attitudes

Fear of invasion stalled the tunnel's progress for many years. Most of the public forgot about the tunnel. Even the tunnel's greatest supporters were having doubts. In 1947, one supporter suggested calling off the entire project. "[Let's] wind up this whole joke," he said.

Luckily, others continued to press forward with the project. Things soon got better. In 1955, the British defense minister declared that a tunnel built under the Channel would pose no danger to England.

Two years later, the Channel Tunnel Study Group was formed. The group sought out plans for a tunnel. In 1959, an engineer named Charles Putnam Dunn

The invention of the tunnel-boring machines gave many Europeans hope that France and England would soon be connected. However, the project's great cost would soon stall it again.

provided the best design. Dunn's plan called for building not one, but three tunnels. Dunn believed this would be the safest way to build. Under the Channel was a layer of rock with many air pockets. Beneath that was a thin layer of solid chalk. This layer was where the tunnel would need to go. Dunn felt one large tunnel would not fit in this narrow space. His design called for two tunnels for railway traffic—one going in each direction. The third tunnel would be a service tunnel. This

tunnel would provide easy access to the main tunnels. It would also improve the flow of air underground.

In 1973, TBMs started digging on both sides of the Channel. However, Britain began to have economic problems. The government had to stop spending money on many things, including the Channel tunnel. On January 19, 1975, the TBMs were buried in the chalk bed. The tunnel project had been put on hold—yet again.

chapter two

Chunnel Vision

The British government insisted that the French take precautions against the problem of rabies. Some Britons felt that animals, such as the red fox, might contract rabies, travel through the Chunnel, and spread the disease across England.

By 1985, the Channel tunnel was back on track. On April 2, the British and French governments sent out a sixty-four-page letter. The letter asked companies to submit plans for building the Channel tunnel. The companies' designs had to follow certain guidelines. The tunnel had to be safe and durable—it needed to last at least 120 years. It also couldn't be an easy target for terrorist attacks. However, one of the guidelines seemed a little odd. The British government wanted the design to prevent animals with rabies from entering the tunnel! Rabies is a disease spread by the bite of infected animals. It attacks the brain and spinal cord, sometimes causing death.

This seemed like a silly concern to some. Rabies hadn't been a serious problem in England since 1922. To many British, though, rabies was no laughing matter. They feared that a rabid animal from France, such as a red fox, might make the long journey across the tunnel. Once on Britain's shores, it might spread its disease far and wide.

Doubtful Designs

Many companies submitted designs. A few designs were truly amazing. Some were just truly bizarre.

Some of the proposed plans to connect England to France were as far-fetched as this bridge design from 1870. Thankfully, others were more serious in nature.

For instance, one plan called for building a bridge across the entire Channel! This bridge would be lifted and held in place by bags filled with gas.

A more serious proposal called for a Channel expressway. In this design, two large tunnels would be built. Most of the time, automobile traffic would travel in the tunnel. Once each hour, however, cars

and trucks would have to halt. At that time, trains would pass through the tunnels.

There were huge flaws in this plan. The tunnels were too big to fit inside the layer of solid chalk. Also, having trains and cars drive into the same tunnel would put travelers' lives at risk. One French railway expert called the idea "completely crazy."

A company named EuroRoute submitted another plan. It combined a bridge and a tunnel. The two would be connected by a spiral ramp, built on top of an island. This plan gained some support. However, most people felt that the complicated design would make drivers nervous. The cost of the plan was also very high.

We Have a Winner

Another company, Eurotunnel, sent in a proposal similar to Charles Dunn's three-tunnel design from 1959. Eurotunnel's plan seemed like the safest bet. If a fire ever broke out in one of the main tunnels, the service tunnel could be used as an escape route. Because the train traffic would only be traveling one way in each tunnel, there would also be no risk of head-on accidents.

In the Eurotunnel plan, only trains would use the tunnel. People wouldn't be able to drive cars through it. However, the trains would be allowed to carry cars from one side of the Channel to the other.

On January 20, 1986, Britain's Prime Minister Margaret Thatcher and France's President François Mitterrand made an exciting announcement. They had chosen the Eurotunnel proposal.

Before workers put the concrete lining of the Chunnel in place, each piece was carefully tested.

Concrete Plans

After a quick celebration, the Eurotunnel group got to work. Their first job was to secure the money that the banks and businesses had promised them.

Transmanche Link (TML) was hired to build the Chunnel. TML had to make several important decisions in a hurry. They had to order the TBMs soon.

It would take more than a year to make these machines and have them delivered to the digging site.

TLM also had to decide the best mix of concrete to use. This concrete would make up the tunnel walls. It was an important

BUILDING BLOCKS

The Chunnel is made up of 674,755 pieces of concrete! During peak production, 144 pieces were made each day.

choice. If they picked a poor mix, chemical compounds in the water called chlorides would seep into the concrete. They would damage the tunnel's protective steel. Over time, this would put the tunnel's structure in danger. Chemists tested several different kinds of concrete. They finally found a perfect mixture of ingredients for the concrete. The ingredients included crushed granite, cement, and fuel ash.

To make enough concrete, TML had to find 1 million tons (1,016,000 metric tons) of granite. Luckily, they located a mountain in Scotland that had a granite center. TML dug out the granite and shipped it to its plant on the Isle of Grain, on the southeast coast of England.

All the concrete for the British side of the tunnels was mixed at this plant. It was a 3-hour trip from the Isle of Grain to the mouth of the tunnel in Folkestone, England. This was the closest place TML could use.

In October 1987, the concrete mixing began. The two towns that would lead to the Chunnel—Calais, France and Folkestone, England—were ready for the dig to begin.

chapter three

Digging In

At 450 tons (457 metric
tonnes) each, just getting
the five TBMs into position
was a tiring task.

Differences of Opinion

French and British leaders had different ideas about how much experience the Chunnel workers needed. The British hired men who had been tunneling for years. The French, however, saw the Chunnel as a chance to give jobs to local men with no tunneling experience. Many of the French workers were desperate for a paycheck. Most of them had never worked on a tunnel before. They had to receive a crash course in training before they could get started.

Home Away From Home

Most of the British tunnelers were not from Folkestone. They needed a place to live while working on the Chunnel. TML built a camp for them called Farthingloe Village. Farthingloe had several living conveniences on the grounds. These included a general store, a barber, and a gym. Tunnelers worked on the Chunnel in 10-hour shifts for six days in a row. They found much-needed relief and comfort at Farthingloe.

Split the Difference

The TBMs on the British side started digging the service tunnel on December 1, 1987. The TBMs were longer than two soccer fields. They could dig at a rate of nearly 250 feet (76.2 m) each day.

The British wanted the service tunnel to be 14.8 feet (4.5 m) in diameter. However, the French had planned for the same tunnel to be 16.4 feet (5 m) in diameter. The British argued that the contract had called for the 4.5-meter size. Any size greater than that would cost more money to build. The French argued that they needed the extra half meter to get their TBMs in and out. There was no way to build the tunnel with two different diameters. Each side had to compromise. They agreed to build the service tunnel with a 15.7 feet (4.8 m) diameter. This satisfied both sides and kept the project moving forward.

In the early stages of building the Chunnel, the two governments often clashed. Each side felt its equipment was the best for the project. The British thought the French followed blueprints and plans too rigidly. The French felt the British didn't plan enough. The French also worried that the Chunnel was being built too quickly. They felt the tunnelers might get sloppy if they felt too rushed.

In Deep

Much of the Chunnel is 150 feet (45.7 m) under the Channel's seabed. It took two and a half hours to descend to the work site. As the tunnel was being

Each day, the workers who helped dig the Chunnel had to go through a long trip. The tunnelers often felt anxious as they made their journey.

built, a system of tracks and seventy work trains took workers and supplies in and out of the tunnel. There were no signals in the tunnels. Men along the tracks talked to the train drivers by radio. If a signal was missed or a radio stopped working, it could have led to a tragic accident.

The energy being produced from the TBMs made the tunnel as hot as a furnace. The temperature was around 100 degrees Fahrenheit (38 degrees Celsius). Fresh water

was constantly sprayed on the machines. This kept them free of dust and saltwater, which would destroy the metal.

However, the water also kept the air sticky and humid. The workers were always covered in sweat. Every worker drank about 12.7 pints (6 liters) of water each day. During the busiest shifts, about 1,000 workers were underground. This means that 5,000 gallons (18,000 l) of water had to be shipped down to them every day.

Something for Everyone

Everyone in the tunnel had an important job to do. TBM operators and engineers made sure the TBMs were working properly. Geologists studied the rock and chalk to make sure the tunnelers were digging in the right places.

Meanwhile, the hand tunnelers used a type of jack-hammer called an air spade to chip away at the chalk. Any hand tunneling in the Chunnel had to be done by the British, since they had the skills to use these tools. The French were not trained to use air spades. It's believed that British hand tunnelers cut about 10 miles (29 km) of tunnel by hand.

TBMs weren't responsible for digging out the entire Chunnel. This tunneler uses an air spade to trim out pieces of chalk.

Once workers struck weak rock, the Chunnel project hit a critical and dangerous point. This tunneler works carefully beside the wet weakened ground.

Problem Solving

In March 1988, the British TBM hit bad ground, or weak rock. Water rushed in around the TBM. It drenched everyone and everything. The railway tracks carrying the men back and forth were buried under streams of water.

The crew always had large pipes near the TBM that could pump water out of the tunnel. Because of this, workers weren't worried about the water. What *did* worry them was what the water would do to the seabed they were digging through. As the TBM drilled, rushing water weakened the layers of rock above it. Giant chunks of heavy rock fell behind the TBM. If one of those chunks fell on a worker, it would crush him.

The men dug 1.2 miles (2 km) deeper, hoping the ground would become stronger. It did not. To deal with the concern of falling rock, a stainless steel hood was developed for the TBM. This hood fit over the TBM, protecting the workers from danger.

Break on Through

On October 30, 1990, the two nations' TBMs came together, at last. The British TBM was driven to the side of the French-dug tunnel.

The workers were joyful after the two sides had broken through. They had done more than connect two nations. They had built a path between dreams of the past and hopes for the future.

Tunnelers on both the French and British side worked to clear the way for the official breakthrough. The ceremony took place on December 1. Phillippe Cozette from France and Graham Fagg from England reached through a hole in the rock. The two men shook hands. Radio stations and TV networks

reported the event. Cameras flashed, preserving the moment. The British manager of the service tunnel, David Denman, was joyful. "[W]e were floating," he said. "We just couldn't believe we'd actually done it." The celebration couldn't last forever, though. There was still work to be done.

chapter four

Laying Tracks

Although England and France had their share of arguments, it was trust and cooperation that helped their project succeed.

Last Minute Problems

With the service tunnel carved out, workers turned their attention to digging the two train tunnels. The project was scheduled to be completed three years later, by mid-1993. However, by March 1993, the trains' signaling system had still not been finished. Without this system, the trains could not safely run through the tunnels.

Eurotunnel and the Safety Authority were arguing over the train cars' emergency doors. The Safety Authority oversaw safety concerns on the Chunnel project. They wanted the safety doors, which pas-sengers could exit from in case of a fire, to be 27.6 inches (70 centimeters) wide. Eurotunnel had designed them to be 23.6 inches (60 cm) wide. The Safety Authority won the argument. The emergency doors had to be redesigned, setting back the Chunnel's progress.

Hand It Over

On December 10, 1993, TML handed over the Chunnel project to Eurotunnel. It was a stormy morning. High winds whipped across the sky. The Channel's seas tossed. That afternoon, two hundred people stood on the platform in Folkestone, England. They were eager to make the first journey in the tunnel to Calais, France. Though the new trains had been completed, they hadn't been fully tested. The Chunnel's first passengers would have to ride on simple British Rail commuter cars.

The Chunnel still wasn't completely finished. Because of this, only one train was allowed in at a time. It was also only allowed to travel 60 miles per hour (100 kilometers per hour). This was much lower than the top speed the Chunnel had been designed for 100 miles per hour (60 kph).

At five o'clock, the French train pulled into and then left the station. One hour and seven minutes later, the British train was allowed to pull away from the station on its journey. A huge celebration in Calais awaited the passengers on the train. Television and film crews covered the event. A jazz band played well into the night.

After the Party

Once the party was over, there was still work to be done in the Chunnel. The brakes on the trains needed to be tested, for instance, and stations along the line needed to be finished. The official opening

Queen Elizabeth II and French President François Mitterrand celebrate the official opening of the Chunnel on May 6, 1994.

ceremony was in May 1994. Full train service wasn't up and running until the summer of 1995.

The Chunnel's final cost was about 15 billion dollars. Thanks to the Chunnel, passengers can travel under the channel's rough seas in 20 minutes.

The Chunnel makes it possible for travelers to get from London to Paris in three hours. During its first six years of operation, more than 57 million passengers rode through the Chunnel. About 12 million tons (12,192,000 metric tons) of cargo were carried through the tunnel. The project brought tourism and jobs to both France and England.

Danger on the Tracks

Each week, dozens of men and women use the Chunnel to chase a dream. However, they aren't regular passengers. Most of these people are refugees who have been forced to leave their own countries. Many of them find shelter at a Red Cross center off the coast of France. This center is located just a mile from the Chunnel's entrance. The refugees often ride illegally on the tops of trains going through the Chunnel. Their journey is an incredibly dangerous one. They hope to become legal residents once they get to England. The Chunnel is filled with hazards such as razor wire and electric fences. In 2001, an Iraqi man was crushed to death by a train while attempting this frightening ride.

Men and women are caught trying to sneak through the Chunnel. They often hope to find better lives in England. Sadly, some of them have died in pursuit of this dream.

This wasn't the only brush with death encountered in the Chunnel. On November 18, 1996, a fire broke out on one of the trains. The emergency was not handled smoothly. Thick smoke found its way into a passenger car. Fans weren't properly turned on for several minutes. Scared passengers lay flat on the

The Chunnel's great success will help link Europeans—and their cities—together for years to come.

floor, choking on fumes. Later, the fans did start working, allowing the smoke to clear. This helped riders to escape to the service tunnel. However, it also fed oxygen into the fire. The flames soared and spread more quickly. It took seven hours for fire-fighters to put out the blaze.

Despite these setbacks, the Chunnel has had a positive impact on Europe. More people are taking

the train instead of a ferry to get between France and England. The Chunnel's service lines will soon expand. TBMs are at work again digging new paths. They are extending the train service that goes through the tunnel to London. The Chunnel has certainly lived up to its billing as a triumph of modern travel. This underground passageway has brought both the nations and people of Europe closer together than ever.

New Words

air spade (**air spayd**) a kind of jackhammer that is used to chip away at rock while building a tunnel

bizarre (bi-**zar**) very strange or odd

bladders (**blad**-urz) organs where waste liquid is stored before it leaves a body

ceremony (**ser**-uh-moh-nee) formal actions, words, and often music performed to mark an important occasion

channel (**chan**-uhl) a narrow stretch of water between two areas of land

chemists (**kem**-istz) persons trained in chemistry

chlorides (**klor**-eydz) chemicals made up of chlorine combined with another element

compressed air (kuhm-**pressd air**) air that has been compressed or squeezed

compromise (**kom**-pruh-mize) an agreement that is reached after people with opposing views each give up some of their demands

diameter (dye-**am**-uh-tur) a straight line through the center of a circle

New Words

durable (**dur**-uh-buhl) tough and lasting for a long time

jackhammers (**jak**-ham-urz) machines used to drill rock, concrete, and similar hard materials

proposal (pruh-**poze**-uhl) a plan or an idea

rabies (**ray**-beez) an often fatal disease that can affect humans, dogs, bats, and other warm-blooded animals

refugee (**ref**-yuh-jee) a person who is forced to leave his or her home because of war, persecution, or a natural disaster

seabed (**see**-bed) the floor of the sea or ocean

signals (**sig**-nuhlz) anything agreed upon to send a message or warning

tunnel-boring machine (TBM) (**tuhn**-uhl **bor**-eng muh-**sheen**) a large, powerful machine that is used to dig a tunnel

For Further Reading

Donovan, Sandra. *The Channel Tunnel*. Minneapolis, MN: Lerner Publishing Group, 2003.

Macaulay, David. *Building Big*. Boston, MA: Houghton Mifflin Company, 2000.

Pollard, Michael. *Roads and Tunnels*. Chicago, IL: Raintree Publishers, 1996.

Resources

Organizations

Channel Tunnel Rail Link
Public Relations
2 Ossulston Street
London
NW1 1HT
www.ctrl.co.uk

Eurotunnel
St Martin's Plain
Cheriton
Folkestone
Kent CT19 4QD
011 44 08705 35 35 35
www.eurotunnel.com

Resources

Web Sites

Great Engineering Feats: The Channel Tunnel

www.teachingtools.com/slinky/tunnel.html
Read about the work that went into building the Chunnel, as well as other great structures, on this Web site.

PBS: Building Big Databank: The Channel Tunnel (Chunnel)

www.pbs.org/wgbh/buildingbig/wonder/structure/channel.html
This Web site has lots of information and fun facts about the building of the Chunnel.

The Channel Tunnel

www.raileurope.com/us/rail/eurostar/channel_tunnel.htm
Learn about the railway that runs through the Channel Tunnel each and every day.

Index

Index

About the Author

Jil Fine visited the Cliffs of Dover many years ago, before France and England were connected. She now writes and lives in Maryland with her husband, who has traversed the Chunnel on a tour of Western Europe.